Carol's Poetry

She dips and disappears into moist earth and water
worlds, a journey rich with vibrant life we cannot see.
Her spirit gathers the ghosts of loved ones passed and
the energy of a kingdom vast.
Her essence is absorbed by the roots of flowers and trees
and tiny creatures of the sea. Seeds are then created and
taken to the air on wings.

Now her spirit is living in the earth, sea and sky, living
and loving in the natural world. She feels every vibration
and pulsation that can be told. Her body anticipates the
spirit's return.
Powerful feelings run through her brain and her heart as
she writes down words to describe the sensations she
feels. We read her words and are transformed by the
birth and magic of Carol's poems.

— *Robert Alan Fryrear*
April 2015

Parables of Passages

Carol Leavitt Altieri

Goose River Press
Waldoboro, Maine

Library of Congress Card Number: 2015957940

ISBN: 978-1-59713-168-1

First Printing, 2016

Cover art by Charlene Vanderslice.

Published by
Goose River Press
3400 Friendship Road
Waldoboro ME 04572
e-mail: gooseriverpress@roadrunner.com
www.gooseriverpress.com

Dedication

For sons Frank Scot and Michael Altieri and Grandchildren:
Jacob, Alyssa, Lianna, Hannah, Michael Jr.,
Joseph, Mark and Mason

In Loving Memory:
Frank Anthony Altieri, April 11, 1932-October 18, 2011
Alicia Ann Altieri, March 4, 1962-August 8, 2008
From: Martha Whitmore Hickman
As I think about my losses, the strands of grief and memory and hope
are mysteriously braided together.

Heritage
Sometimes when depression's long night
ended and I could move beyond
sorrow's thrall, I wondered if guardian
angels had rescued me from closet
caves where I curled up to seek
safety in dark corners hidden
from hideous monsters spawned
by neglect in abandonment's lair.

I pay homage still to angels
but acknowledge ancestors too
who conquered prairies, planted grain,
sang into my blood Beowulf's songs,
sowed their Viking seeds in commands
to stay, stand, slay my Grendels.
From: Patricia Barone

Special Thanks

I would like to thank all my fellow poets for helping me bring the poems into their final forms. Sincere gratitude to all who gave encouragement and stimulated me in many ways and who have been unfailingly helpful, Guilford Poetry Guild members: Audrey Fitting, Gwen Gunn, Julie Harris, Margaret Iacobellis, Karen Johnson, Nancy Meneely, Jane Muir, Pat O'Brien, and Gordy Whiteman.

My profound thanks to Gemma Mathewson who beautifully took some of the photographs used in the book. Also, I'm so grateful to the talented Charlene Vanderslice from Ocean Benefit Paintings, a water advocate artist who painted the Breaking Through swimming turtle.

My deepest and continual thanks to Edwina Trentham for being a poet of wonders, a true original, for stimulating valuable prompts and strong creative support and critiques as the poetry book took shape. She gave me many real sparks of illumination.

Many grateful thanks for my summer poetry workshop led by Edwina Trentham and fellow poets, including Barbara Batt, Gwen Gunn, Pat O'Brien, Karen Torop, Patricia Barone, Janet Greenberg, Sherry Horton, Lauren Rhines, Jay Thumar and Mary Volk.

Much appreciation to Frank Scott, who very patiently and generously assisted me with technical support services. His continual guidance made my life easier in so many ways.

In addition, my adult children, Frank and Michael, granddaughters, Alyssa, Lianna, and Hannah; grandsons, Michael, Joseph and Mark who inspired me to greater insights with accomplishments, interests and disciplined work, who have supported me emotionally all the years and kept me going when I felt the binding thread of loss and grief.

Contents

I
New Hampshire Family Farm//1

Woodland Ephemerals//5

My Father When Young//7

Head in Hands//9

My Father Teaches Me Astronomy//10

The Swimming Pond//12

Nature's Wide-Screened Light Show//14

Horse and Buggy Egg Man//15

The Sky Is Falling with Perseids//17

Living Outside Our Solar System//18

Hammonasset Nurturing//20

Sunday School in the Country//22

A Light Shines Here//23

Ode for the Family Reunion//25

Contents

What the Blizzard Brought//26

The Line Workers//29

Maple Sap to Syrup//30

Finding an Antique Bird Book from Childhood//32

II
Staying Overnight in the Woods//33

In Central Park//35

Painted Buntings//37

Scoping All Night in New Zealand//38

My Shakespeare's Orchard//39

The Garden on the Ledge//41

Baptism by Neapolitan Fire Pit//43

Pilgrimage to Beatrix Potter's Farms//44

Pilgrimage to New Zealand//45

Tale of the Half-Mad Deer Stalker//48

Contents

The Broadening Sky//51

The Rugged Shore//52

Other-Worldly Creatures//53

Seasonal Changes//55

Viewing "The Starry Night" by Vincent Van Gogh//57

After the Earthquake and Tsunami Roared Over Japan//58

III
This Little Piggy//59

Expedition to the Domain of Secrets in Papua, New Guinea//61

Hammonasset Coast//63

Wandering in Hammonasset Park//65

Gathering American Chestnuts//67

Now That She Is Gone//68

Old Man Reminiscences, 1845//69

Letter to My Lover//71

Contents

First Love//73

In the Evening//75

Love Lies Bleeding//77

Forgetting How to Sing Without Him//78

Sitting Outside Starring at Flowers//80

Fracking Despair//82

Dancing at Donahue's//84

Kennewick Man Speaks Secrets After 9,000 Years//85

Learning to Dance with the Shakers//87

Last Year//89

Inner Dresden//90

As I Ebb Toward...//91

Here's a Portrayal of a Woman I Know//93

Retreat to the Cabin//94

Contents

Bald Cypress in Florida Park//95

Farmer Roscoe (The Philosopher) ca 1937...//96

The Spirit Bear, Panda of Canada//98

Gingko, Oldest Surviving Plant//99

Finding the Gingko Tree//100

The Lost Girls, Men and Babies//101

His Story of Eighteen//103

Remaining Destination//104

The First Things I Remember
New Hampshire Family Farm 1940-1954
Thirteen Ways

I
Sunup to sundown in the Bible country, the old man of the
mountain gazes over his denizens. In the universe of
trees and animals, my father journeys. He puts on the harness of
labor over strong hands, leg and arm muscles and plants a
hundred apple, cherry, pear and peach trees on the farmland.

II
Camel-colored Guernseys and spotted Holsteins salivate for
water, grass and grain. I unhitch their stanchions and shepherd
them out to pasture. One unfazed by my attention runs away
into woods, the others follow me with satin-looking eyes. They
watch me, a cow whisperer. When rich grasses grow in spring,
cows thrash in shallows, chomp sweet roots and forge alliances.

III
My blood pulses to the farm's rhythm as a pregnant cow
disappears. I pray her calf will not be marked for slaughter.
Cresting the hill, the cows are coming home clustered in groups.
Some nuzzle me and I groom their coats.

IV
 Mother Guernsey cow stands in a single-minded vigil over her
new-birth calf.

V
Royal-blue barn swallows tumble from the sky and return to
nesting colony, mouths loaded with bugs, for nestlings.
Every day chickens run up the ramps and settle into their beds. I
pick freshly laid eggs from under Rhode Island Reds. Foxes came
in the night and snatched some chickens. I'm reminded of the folk
song, *Oh the fox goes out in the town tonight and waits for the moon
to give him light....*

VI
When my father takes some eggs to incubate, I don't want to see
baby chicks change to be hens and roosters. Gracing the gardens,
older hens cluck and roosters crow most of the day pecking tiny
bugs from the hay and weeds. They scratch the ground, not
vigilant. A red-tailed hawk swoops down.

VII
Woodchuck and skunks find homes, dig burrows beneath the
barn and I spread fox urine granules to scare them away. I trot
away from the clacking geese home-security agents who peck my
legs.

VIII
The palomino saddle horse and the workhorse chase each other in
the pasture and the wild one gallops away, jumping the five-foot
fence.

IX
My father, sister and I deliver apples, milk and eggs from a white
horse and a red wagon.

X
Flowers in the grasslands jostle one another, a linear thrust
toward the heart of May. Hellebores, snow drops, daffodils and
narcissi expand their empires and spread over the dandelion
weeds.

XI
June morning, I tear off my jacket and socks, run through
clinging vines, hayfields and sassafras trees.

XII
Then I stand like a beech tree holding tan leaves from last year
that didn't drop away. Here under the canopy, soaring into
dizzying spirals, feel the breath of wings and swing of rain into
sun.

XIII
My aunt, sister and grandparents are the celestial stars revolving
around the heavens in the night sky. I look for the moon,
Jupiter, and Venus lined up in their orbits.

Woodland Ephemerals

My father brings a bouquet to me,
most treasured, newly-sprouted wild flowers.
In April, sweet fragrance from forest edge,
 like rarity of yellow lady slippers.

Mayflowers trailing leathery leaves and woody stems
peek and push from earth,
hiding under heart-shaped leaves.
The earliest, tinged pink, spread their petals,
perfumed and spry, ushering in spring.

Mayflowers lead the way for azaleas, columbines,
 trilliums, Quaker-ladies, and Solomon's seals.
All join the woodland show,
bowing like courtiers before a queen.
While looking, I hear rills and ripples
of the Isinglass River.

Breathe deeply and inhale the fragrance
symbolizing deep unspoken love.
In shady places of clumps and patches,
flowers commingle with earth
scent and apple blossom essence.

In heaven now, my father clutches
a bouquet of Mayflowers.
Some wildflowers linger
in pockets of mind.
I cultivate their sanctuaries for retreat.

My Father When Young

My dad didn't say much about his boyhood
when we lived on the farm in Flag Hill
but my Aunt Florence used to tell me
that he was born to make others laugh and sing:
 playing the harmonica and singing
 on the lawn swing late in the night
 under moon rays, as fire flies flashed.

In those old days, blizzards swept across fields
and he snow shoed over ten-foot high snow banks.
The sleigh he was riding on the way to school tipped over
 when his horse spooked
 and he prayed to avoid the *whack whack*
 of teacher's ruler in the back cloakroom.

 My aunt told stories of other years about how he got lost
in woods and wetlands, climbed trees, scooped up frogs,
picked up a snapping turtle by its tail to scare the girls.
 Another time he paddled his canoe in the river
 as thunderheads crashed. Negotiating swirls, his canoe
 swamped and he lost all his school books, afraid
 to return to school.

At fourteen, he loved taking people for rides
in his make-shift truck,
 jerry-rigged out of other car parts
 and drove his horse-drawn wagon
 gathering scrap for liberty ships.

7

A boy of woods and friendships, surveying
his small town domain, he made a fort in the scaffold
of an old maple tree,
      a resting perch for fellow tree dwellers
      secure in the high boughs; cared for it with his hands
      and thick hedges of power.

Head in Hands

Inspired by Lisa De Lippi's painting

I'm seeing a painting of a friend, I know well.
He is not an ordinary man. His mind is unsettled
by reading two newspapers, *Wall Street Journal*
and the *New York Times*.
Violent hurricanes, tsunami and tornado winds thrash city
and countryside.

What powerful forces uprooted him and sent him
out into the world?
His mother and father held high expectations
as a second-generation first son and supported him richly.
Yet, he *started working when only thirteen*, he liked to say.

His face is deeply- grooved and the anguish remains there
from the loss of another one he loved more than all on earth.
Was it defeat, despair or anger that I watched?

He walked alone with the aching desolation
of the land thinking about what was left and lived
in the shifting scenes of his garden and domestic life.
Something within him died-spirit and passion
but still he poured the foundations
for others as always he had done.

He often wondered if his roots had reached
and spread deep and wide enough.

My Father Teaches Me Astronomy

After the campfire dies down,
on a Mars/Jupiter or/Mercury evening, my dear dad
leads me. We make our way under a seductive gibbous moon.
He loves to say,
If the moon shows a silver shield,
be not afraid to reap your yield.

The sky incandescent converges with stars.
Dad and I pull constellations in with our binoculars
as he tells me about the pictures ancients saw in the sky
and makes up some of his own. He raises his arm to point
out the brightest stars.

Light flares and flickers, the right time to find
the ethereal Northern Cross.

Cepheus and his Queen Cassiopeia on a tilted throne
rush in to yield transcendent clusters.
Perseus, the hero protects
the chained maiden, Andromeda
from Taurus, the bull. I am starry-eyed.

Glowing in the sky, the great musician Orpheus
plays the lyre.
Dad tells me to face north,
and I'm enchanted to see the Seven Sisters.
In time's infinite blaze, as partners we watch Perseid
meteor showers, hundreds, ephemeral, ignite the sky,
each hour moving toward the earth.

As I idolize Dad, we continue east into the great square
of Pegasus, the handle of the Big Dipper circles resplendent.

If you ever get lost in the woods, follow Ursa Minor
home by Polaris, the North Star, Dad reminds me.

The Swimming Pond

In misty land of memory
every spring and summer,
down the dirt road from father's farm
we bathed after haying
washing our hair with floating homemade soap.

Flag Hill Pond born of snow melt
from Kersage Mountain
encircled by sumac, nettles, and poison ivy.
Around us, in hay fields Holstein cows chewed
pasture grass and horses galloped freely.

Neighbors' boys pitched themselves down
from branches.
When I plunged in shrieking from sudden cold,
they splashed and bullied me.

I worried about pushing the bullies off,
the waves burying me
and snapping turtles on the bottom.
Our private swimming pond
isolated in the mountain landscape.

I ran up the bank and dove in again
sometimes belly flopping.
At times, swift currents propelled me around in
my inner tube that tipped me over.
When boys ducked me, I popped up
from darkness of tannic-colored water.
I mastered swimming here with many plunges
and caught my breath when I was ducked under.

I wonder was our pond the hidden trail to another
life that moved on, spiraling in circles and uphill climbs
like clearing a rock strewn New Hampshire field?

Nature's Wide-Screen Light Show

Whispered about in darkness,
mystery ancients recorded
in sacred books, written in logs of forgotten ships
sunk to the bottom.

Early settlers saw the lights as gay
polka dancers and Athabaskans of Alaska watched
sky dwellers, spirits of the dead sending
messages.

Shared with friends across midnight, they came
to watch aurora borealis in the deepest, coldest
regions of the planet's reach of space. In wonder,
their eyes opened to the night sky as gossamer rays unfold.

Lime-colored and bright-magenta rays flashed
and flickered — erratic as the wind. Incandescent
meteors of northern lights blazed and swayed in display.
They ebb and follow some unseen authority,
power humans will never command.

Faster than eyes can follow, behind shadows
of mountains, the event exploded above them, colors
like drapes dashing and sweeping. The hunters
felt communion across the ages with travelers
and mystics who were stunned and awestruck
by ghostly lights in the sky.

The aurora illuminated the moon hanging
over the mountains.
Bright waves of light shimmering around the sky faded
into the heavens through the shroud of mist.

Horse-and-Buggy Egg Man

Bert from Northfield
doing the work of four
started out at dawn as my father and I
used to do, not so long ago.

> The sun melted
> blankets of fog
> on the river and pastures
> in Merrimack County.

Even though snow piled on the ridge
this crackling-wind day,
he drove his ancient,
blue milk cart
with red wooden wheels
every season
hearing the soughing of pines
and oak trees dropping acorns in lowlands.

> He takes eggs and vegetables to town
> winding through Northfield across the river
> downtown, stopping at houses,
> fire station, post office, and nursing homes.
> Door after door, cartons of eggs jostle
> in his wagon until he has delivered all.

Now after seventy years, he's brought more
than one-hundred dozen cleaned and weighed eggs
every day
with his dutiful horse, Mischief
clip-clip-clopping along.

Last year the buggy rolled over him
and broke his ribs.
Still, Bert hangs on for dear life,
trudging out to his barn, pigsty, and hen
house, all he ever needs.

The Sky Is Falling with Perseids

I climb Kearsage and wait with children
in celestial August time, before the new Moon
to see fireworks from the mountain top.
One hundred million, trillion, gazillion
meteors, sky years distant descend
the atmosphere uniting and showering
over all watchers on the planet Earth.
I, with the children wonder about the nurseries
where stars are being born and all of us aligned
to the Moon swelling toward the full.

Jupiter, Venus and Mercury converge
close to the horizon. I see a vision
that all celestial bodies revolve over me.
Imagine how infinitesimal
my life, how tiny my home is
against the depth and breadth of the heavenly scale.

Living Outside Our Solar System Sestina

We earthlings launch a ship into space
searching for planets capable of life
that could sustain humans. Our solar
system astronomers are Promethean
and do not want a mammon payoff, but only
the gratification of joining a community of planets

with scientists, gods, historians and other planets
non-earth-like. Our space ship travelling in outer space
will safely transport us and then we will gather only
some prebiotic soup and comets we need to live life,
nothing more than what the Greek titan, Prometheus
and other gods need of fire, water and air from our solar

system. We think there are worlds in our solar
system that have the same size and distance our planet
from its stars. If found, other gods with Prometheus
could model better humans from clay, teach space
agriculture and arts of civilization and creative life,
all that is unlike earth, so thriving and vigorous, not only

what we now know of earth but primitive bacteria not only
like what geysers at Yellowstone show us, but solar
ultraviolet light on the surface of a living
comet, such as proteins, sugars, amino acids on the planet.
Alas, we are just a speck of dust in our galaxy of space.
We yearn for other habitable planets that Prometheus

in his Christ-like way in art and creativity, as Prometheus
in his hubris trying to push power and freedom not only
to godlike extremes but sacrificing himself as well in space
as the nearby stars in our universe's solar
system in our galaxy in the midst of our planet.
For us humans, we will find places that can support life.

It's possible there are other forms of life
that can beam our presence with help of Prometheus.
Proserpina could step in to help him on a new planet
by bringing spring and planting vegetation, not only
in our galaxy but with extraterrestrial life in solar
systems of immense distances between stars in space.

Only before this year passes, we are going to live life
with Janus looking forward to thresholds of planets
inspired by Prometheus—in full solar space.

Hammonasset Sestina

Near Purple Martin pond, plants sprout,
while along the Moraine Trail among the rocks
yellow-rumped warblers scurry the leaves.
As we bird watch there, I scatter seeds to nourish
them for nesting. I am blessed to be close to home
drawing the honey down along the Sound, the place to live.

How can I ever move away from my second home
intimate as I am with each contour and every leaf,
the diverse creatures living among the rocks,
teaching us lessons about every species alive.
The naturalists do not weed but help withered sprouts
to grow. In shallow water during high tide, kelp nourishes

crabs. Sea anemones change each day to be nourished
where they grow adding erect arms to move their homes.
They thrust themselves out of the sea like groping sprouts
and change their shapes among glistening leaves
of sea lettuce that need chlorophyll to keep alive
as stalks of finger sponges attach to rocks.

Large flocks of red knots comb the shores feeding on rocks.
whose growth horseshoe crabs' eggs can heartily nourish.
Farmers and friends brought this Edenic garden alive
where foxes, shorebirds and owls grope for a home
as other winter creatures camouflage under leaves.
Some plants lie in wait until spring, mysterious sprouts.

Armadas of jelly fish sprout pennants on tentacles
among rocks as seaweed, stems and leaves nourish life.
While alive, I cannot leave my Hammonasset home.

Sunday School in the Country

Five miles over the rocky and sandy road, I trudged
to a farm house for Vacation Bible School;
a minister and his wife and three children presided.

As I walked along, I loved the tall Joe-Pye Weed flowers
in bloom skirting the country road. The fragrance of green needles
leaves and wildflowers was pervasive.

A god existed in the roadside plants
with butterflies and bees, sipping and sucking nectar.
A commune of goats idled in the pasture on the way.

Mostly, mother made me go, though I sometimes hid
in the forest. There were stresses on my parents' marriage
and I would rather be with friends in the village.

I tried very hard to pray for God's deliverance.
and grasped the view that God would support me.
We settled in the cluttered house with the minister and his wife.

As I was a hard-working child, she told me,
"With Jesus you will always have money!
And you will not have to work so hard doing the farm chores."

The minister's wife gave quarters for every Bible verse
memorized and a seal to stick on a ribbon. I memorized
as fast as I could and never did forget the 23th Psalm.

A Light Shines Here

From: 1985 Photo of Wonalancet Union Chapel, New Hampshire, 1880
with White Mountain National Forest in the background.

A burst of white as the church stands
surrounded by laurel on the edge of the woods.
A wood thrush above in a sheltering tree
sings out his rich vesper song:
Come to me, come to me, I am here, I am here!
In this tiny world of a larger universe,
music echoes like the call of the brook that runs down
the mountain's range. Immortal lichen and moss spread
on the rocks so the darkness won't fall too heavily.

The iridescence of the church reflects the ivory
of time-tested faith strengthened
over hundreds of years.

I step into a soft and silvery retreat
from a great spool of the sun's natural light.

Inside there is a kind of seamstress of souls,
senders and receivers of earth and star energies,
the intermediaries between our world
and the invisible one of another.
I hear the angels sing
as they collect the life force
and spread it panoramically into the kingdom.

Ode for the Family Reunion

One October morning, from fifty states,
ancestors arrived, roots nourished first
in Plymouth Rock.
Granted a petition from the Meeting House
as belfry bells chime. Auspicious spirits
fly in and out of wide-spreading trees.
Here they muster amid cedar saplings.

Nine acres expand to oak-hickory-pine woods.
Some fallen pines where settlers
once planted gardens, built cabins,
pastured Guernseys and Holsteins.

Descendents of families moved westward,
and Mormons became the chosen government.
The flags we raise in honor. I remember my forbears
carried by hearses and horse wagons, placed in the ground
and my throat burns and heart heaves.
Pulling our divining rods,
some relatives want to return.

The drummer beats to arms. We listen
to genealogy levitating from Ye Olde Burial Grounds.
Historians deep search in the sanctum
as members promise repair of cemetery stones
mottled with lichens.

What the Blizzard Brought

I'm stocking the winter feeding stations in bleakest weather
amidst the snow as the wild birds come seductively from the
labyrinth of the boreal forests. Piercing
the winter winds,
flocks of black-capped chickadees, acrobatic foragers cling upside
down to the swinging feeder.

Faithful in all weather, visiting every day, little downy woodpeck-
ers brave the fresh falling snow
with well-designed bodies,
in a black and white military coat of feathers, under red-tagged
hammerheads. Most incessantly, they peck away clinging sideways
to the suet cage.

Joining the coalition, in roller-coaster flight, American goldfinches,
now in buff-to-olive garb flutter past my red-hooded head, when
most of their relatives have fled south to the tropics with their
wealth of gold.

Adding to the full array, with a prolonged trill of whistling notes,
the solitary winter wren- short tail pointing upwards comes out
of hiding from the tree hole, lively
and active as a June bug flicking
from branch to branch.

Withstanding the perils of wind chill,
landing on mounds of snow, slate-colored juncos and white-
breasted nuthatches begin singing all at once, each with wavering
voices on a different key.

As I take leave, arcing around
to the other side of the house,
a parliament of white-throated
sparrows render
Old Sam Peabody, as they hasten
on calling,
We survived another godforsaken flight!

Crashing the festival, driven by hunger,
a sharp-shinned hawk with a hair raising shriek,
kee-eeee-arrr, kee-eeee, arrr returns
to his hunting grounds and all the birds flee,
flying away to protected woods -enough
of them to make the frosty air
suggestive-darkening and brightening
all at once.

The Line Workers

With *Frankenstorm* northeaster,
I had a snug bed to fall in as the storm thrashed.
Hundreds of others battered,
and flooded, struggled to stay
on the split earth when a caravan of international
line workers in reflective yellow vests flew in.

Workers who travelled thousands of miles
huddled in tents, slept on cots
and struggled like the hands
of Baal. They motored Zodiacs and waved flashlights
as the sky turned roguish with gale force winds.

The mutants of extreme weather
skirted sharpened hurricane winds and rustling rain.
Self-lit, they worked beyond sunset as the moon shone
a glowing night light on window glass.
Sand from beach dunes grew in volume,
spread crystals and flecks that tumbled
and caught light.
Bucket brigades pumped big bubbles of hot air
like lava lamps.

Gazing in astonishment at nature's spectacle,
mighty giants cascaded in polyphony
of voices piercing the raging winds
trying to help those shivering in the dark.

They lighted burning flares along pitch-black streets.
As darkness and winds stretched for days, they remained.
Who knows that this rescue mission shut homes
to their families' survival?

Maple Sap to Syrup

The image overflows
as my father standing in front of the sleigh,
as Sandy our work horse pulls ahead.

In March, we drilled holes, drove in metal spigots,
hanging a collecting bucket under each
as saplings responded with sweetness.

Twisting over winding paths,
our horse shuddered from the cold
and shook off the snow flakes.

We revered red buds bristling from rugged slopes.
Between the outer bark and heartwood,
sap flowed from upper limbs to holding tanks
Forty gallons of sap for one sweet syrup.
Crows cackled their curiosity.

Colossi of sugar maple trees connected
by underground roots. Firing vats by hand-split wood,
maybe dad was resolved
to make an abundance this year.
Yet, there was no profit in our liquid gold,
only a promise for all those hours of labor.

I like to think as we went about collecting sap
my father remembered childhood joys
of waffles, pancakes and "sugar on snow,"
true to his New Hampshire nature.

Finding an Antique Bird Book from Childhood

You, book of nature led me to a secret hiding place
above the cows and horses in the barn
where I heard the voices call from the fields
to become a bird-land lover.
You guided me to the choreography of barn
swallows and I came breast to breast with
their royal blue and brown plumage.
I learned their music and followed secret jaunts
to other nests. In the witching hour before breakfast
you took me out to the rolling country
interlaced by brooks and streams
to birds of passage that I wouldn't meet again
until next season.

Mirabile dictum!! The bird- quest helped me choose
to get on speaking terms with the champion
family of sparrows. I made them all my main subjects:
the song sparrow singing first in the back yard,
the chipping sparrow enhanced with spring vestments,
the salt-marsh sparrow that could balance on a stalk
and the field sparrow singing a hymn at evening.

You led me to a love for all meanings
and seasons of nature under heaven,
grateful for what I've learned and what I haven't…

Staying Overnight in the Woods

We kindle light in our faces
visiting the darkening woods
where Hester Prynne shed her shame.

The neon-pink sun sinks and the night reigns
over the pine trees. We scan the eastern
sky and find the glowing Milky Way
sweeping in an arc and trust it
to guide us, as it once did the sailors
navigating the high seas.

Our pillows, a roll up of moss and ferns
next to ground pine and running cedar.
Like Shakespeare's characters we
magically shed our identities.

We sleep in the crisp, cool air
saturated by the fragrance
of night-blooming primroses.

The sanctuary bewitches us with the scent
of early love. We meet the painted turtles
who stare at us with greenish eyes.

Feeling a hushed awe, we linger
beyond the edge of wilderness.
Your voice is etched into cairns of memory.

In Central Park Gardens

*It will be nice to have the whole world in one place, one field,
living and growing together in harmony.*

— Yoko Ono

Wilderness and civilization flow into each other,
surrounded by honking buses,
throbbing cars, flashing trucks, horse-
drawn carriages, policemen on horseback
and joggers on foot paths.

Everything is vital: *Harlem Meer*
stocked with fish near *Huddlestone Bridge*.
Clouds ruffle the blue sky as a cardinal
with a brand of grass in its beak helps a
mate build a nest beneath azaleas.

Turtles with backs shaped for beauty grasp
for passing flies as they sun on undulating
shoreline of the pond.

On Monument's Plaza children throng
to play King of the Hill and climb
over Alice in Wonderland's toadstools.
Here, Shakespeare in a contemplative mood
stands over his woodland gardens.

Masterpieces-within-masterpieces,
sermons in stones, reflected in waters,
curvilinear drives and meandering paths,
and keys that open locked gates forever.

The Ramble on the ravine, with
birdwatchers in front of skyscrapers, no
trees could ever camouflage.

Nearby the Duke Ellington statue soars
by the streetlights on the Mall immersing
crowds where harmonious accord pervades.

We amble at sunset onto the Bow Bridge.
The sky changes from smoky-blue
to royal-blue as city's lights glimmer.

Across from the Dakota,
Yoko Ono's *Strawberry Fields*, strewn
with rose petals to honor John Lennon.
Here, imagine a peaceful world and Jordan's
fothagilla growing next to Israel's cedar.

The *IMAGINE* medallion,
memorial to those who've died untimely.
All earth's friends with nothing left out.

Painted Buntings

I search for a Painted Bunting along the southeast seaboard
hardly knowing how exotic and gaudy they are.
Spotting my first, he flashes from tree to brushy thickets,
showing off his bloodstone red breast, brilliant-green wing
        patches
and lapis-lazuli helmet. So streamed with colors I think
Remedios Varo must have painted it for her *Creation of the Birds*.
And when the Painted Bunting flings out its notes
it pours for us a rich libation that sounds across the river.

Greek mythology tells us that the princess Scylla was transformed
into this beautiful bird when she drowned after King Minos
spurned her. With all the time and distance between then and
        now,
today Painted Buntings are targets for poachers of caged birds.
When partners are caged, you can imagine the heartbroken
woe and sense of loss when the other is left behind.

Scoping All Night for a Kiwi in New Zealand

Tribute to Mike Lennon

In mountainous Maori country,
we seek the scarce kiwi whose mottled
brown plumage blends perfectly with the understory.

Flightless birds build nest burrows months
in advance so moss and ferns can grow over.

I settle in for a long wait in the nook of a mossy stump
and doze. Awakened, I patrol for a kiwi that sleeps
all day in a hollow log.

The forest, silent and still
is shattered by a male kiwi
with a noisy outburst from a long curved bill.
It stirs itself, snuffles around,
announces departure
for night's hunt of worms, grubs and berries.

I imagine the female sitting for 75 days
with the egg inside her,
so large it leaves no room for food.

I'd like to stroke the female's belly for her relief
and wish for the round, spiky kiwi chick
to emerge into a bird-loving world.

A kiwi's call sounds like a last gasp
of a vanishing species
in a once avian Eden.

My Shakespeare's Orchard

I miss walking down the lane
feeling a southwest wind breathing
with gentle rain drops falling
as I found my way to the apple orchard.
Hundreds of trees were planted
by my father years ago.
Over full green fields, trees thrust out crimson buds
and pink blossoms suffused sweet perfume.

In the orchard I listened to the convention
of blue birds, my eyes-blinking;
one male with bright orange breast clung
to the cavity entrance of the nest box defying
house wrens and English sparrows.

Here and there, as I stooped down to gather
some blue Quaker ladies and meadow buttercups,
a peacock butterfly passed over my hands.

In October, fall palpitated on the scene
as arbor of trees yielded a wealth of golden
and crimson apples. Tossed out of the house,
my sisters and I gathered bushels
climbing the spreading branches
surveying vistas of Kearsage Mountain.
The fragrant sweet scent lured the hawk
moth pollinators.
This memory sharp as a blade
on my father's whetstone wheel.

The Garden on the Ledge

I'm half lost in my garden of many sun risings,
in the field among lemon-colored blossoms
that sprawl like bristles of a hand brush.
In clumps, other pearl petals caress and gleam.

Filled with the harbor's breeze, I rock in my chair
near Adam's Needle* that emerges from brick-like soil.
Around, wild moss vignettes mound like moguls.
I wonder at a handful of earth and what it holds
and watch the seeds break their bonds and rise.

The sun dipping down sparks the garden
and loosens the faint, sweet perfume of flowers.
Petals of the carmine poppies spread out like wings
of cherubs. Seeds blow like shuttlecocks
and whirl in the wind.
It is the time of the shapeless slugs that eat by night
and hide by day. They fold the buds splendor
into their tiny hearts.
Farther out, a bee blunders into a gush
of a wood thrush's music.

Clover and crab grass fasten
themselves into soil. One hand holds the stem
in sunshine and roots grasp the soil in darkness.
Tufts of fern in clefts of rocks mingle leaves
and go undisturbed.

*The common name of a Yucca plant because of its spiny leaves.

Baptism by Neapolitan Fire Pit

I
Just past the swimming pool edge
and where the lawn used to be, a recruitment
of strong relatives dig up the back
yard hoisting the wheel barrow
and hauling paving stones.
The leader knows the protocol
cobbling lava rocks
into perfect wood fire design
for family's and friends' gatherings.

With the blend of reverence and creation,
he lays down the landscaping fabric
and circular seating fills the round of his knowing.
Lava rock stabilizes the base and he uses bricks
to build a pit and install a grate for the stove.

2
The godfather, envisioning his father,
pursued his apprenticeship manning the oven.
His daughters measure with meticulous zeal
for the perfect Neapolitan pizza.
One daughter spreads olive oil around the mozzarella,
sprinkles the basil and tops
with rich-grown garden tomatoes. `

The tempting scents of margarita
and marinara waft more pungent
than I could imagine.
Lips press against original pizzas.
And the rising crust becomes the back yard.

Pilgrimage to Beatrix Potter's Farms

So take the time and follow me, in April, May or June.
Lift the stile and cross over the wall to admire
the wide Lake District landscape.
Windermere streams dip with morning mist
turning pale rose under the sun.
Snow drops run wild,
elbow their way into the clot-of-gold crocuses.
Return to your childhood and motherhood
of fairy caravans,

Flopsy, Mopsy, Jemima Puddle-duck,
Tommy Tiptoes and Peter Rabbit raid carrots.
There's a scene in the wildflower meadow
that we could paint, grand open woodlands
full of noble trees. Upon the fells, the wild daffodils
grace the torrent of azaleas down into the valley
and up to the farms. Beatrix Potter plants
for each season: pansies and peas, foxgloves
and columbine, black currents and strawberries.
Here, the seasons ferment like a crock of cider.
Pluck some apples from her trees in the orchard.
Then come with me to watch the herds
of Herdwick sheep and hear cuckoos
call from the woods. The sun warms the witch hazel
with its astringent spicy scent.
Let us watch as Potter pours her heart
into every animal, fruit and flower.

Pilgrimage to New Zealand

Sun lights the pathway funneling
into Mount Cook Lilies and buttercups.

Wood warblers glean and gyre
from blossoms along streams

and chorus frogs begin vesper songs
along the ridge and up the gorge

of canyons and hollows. The Parson
Bird's throat swells with mimics, clicks

and bell-like sounds as it makes an aerial
dive pursuing a weakened gecko.

Sundew, star flowers, mountain daisies
entangle. Silver-green lichens trace

a lacy palette on rocks and boulders.
Muffled roar of a river flowing

to the sea drowns a glacial valley
eroding its core . Distant kauri trees,

ten feet tall, when Jesus walked the land
provide the pagoda tiers casting shadows

over tree ferns. Across marshland,
little blue heron, one leg resting in shallow

slough searches out hidden fish
and mayflies in swirling current.

Honor every creature for its
act of artifice to prevail.

Tale of the Half-Mad Deer Stalker

It is the time
of the hungry herd that visit early morning
and gorge all day and night.
They fold our plants' splendor into their hearts and bodies.

The whole extended family
of does and fawns at their physical peak.
The bucks, tall and graceful sport sleek
grayish-brown coats and branching antlers.
The dress of does and fawns glow glossy tan
and bucks' antlers grow longer consuming
my hard-earned feast.

The pack loiters in the yard,
look around for clearance, grunt
and then devour prickly holly shrubs,
ravage the day lilies shearing off
all the golden blossoms.

I watch a doe with hollow stomach chomp
impatiens and ravage my struggling perennials
leaving purple and ruby translucent petals
with sun shining through.

Backyard deer multiply and overstep boundaries.
No coyotes or bobcats can take them down.
Half mad, I run out with a rake and try
to scare them away.

Does and bucks lunch on junipers, graze on the viburnam,
and fill up on rich, green-blue hosta,
snipping off the sweet-scented
spice bush. They flip their white tails as fawns raise
large brown eyes and shear off the rest of the garden.

The Broadening Sky

The White Mountains
were ablaze with golden, green and russet richness
when my father lost his grocery store in Nova Scotia.

> We moved to New Hampshire in 1942
> in a Chevrolet truck with our scant
> furniture and footlockers. My family

welcomed to a new land
known as the *Live Free or Die* state.
We settled on a farmstead of one-hundred

> acres: farmhouse, orchards, pasture
> and woodlands. During mud season we needed
> muck boots to push and free the truck

stuck up to its axle. Another traveler
with a horse, rescued us and helped jack it out.
Among the blue, wild spring Quaker Ladies,

> rocks and boulders propagated the open pastures.
> A moose in winter coat of chocolate brown
> stood knee deep in the ice-melting river .

Startling me, he soon vanished into the tangled briars
of the advancing darkness and left his hoof prints deep
on the wetted earth.

> As I gazed at the evening sky, Mars, Jupiter and Mercury
> were visible with Orion, the hunter wearing a three-star
>   belt.
> See the constellations that revolve across the sky?

The Rugged Shore

Inspired by Tony D'Amico's painting,
Off the Coastline of New England

Hike the land to fulfill a lasting bond
with the peninsulas' finger tips
and fjord estuaries.
Fresh water of the Sheepscot River shimmies
its tentacles to Muscongus Bay near the Yankee
fishing village.
Links of islands reach out one ahead of the other
trailing bittersweet red berries and sea- foam green
bayberry scents.

After the coniferous forest, pass under a swing bridge
and leave behind a pain-riven world. Walk
on terraced steps, sample blueberries along the path.
Close to thunder hole, hear the boom of the sea
against the boulder-piled, jagged shoreline.

In the rime on intertidal rocks, barnacles feather out
and tiny crabs scuttle to shelter in red seaweed.
When sunset comes, gaze at the deep-blue bay.
Listen to the hermit thrush's harmony
and try not to leave this
place of paradox where she is waiting.

Other-Worldly Creatures in an Acoustic Storm

For thou didst cast me into the deep,
Into the heart of the seas,
And the flood was round about me;
All thy waves and billows passed over me.

—Jonah 2:3

Our ship rolls roughly in ocean swells.
Off the coast of the Pacific Ocean
humpbacks and sperm whales
with deep set eyes cavort in pods.
Bubbles flow from blow holes.
In the nurturing bath of the sea, dorsal fins knife
through water as pectoral fins glide past.
Announcing their positions,
humpbacks sing arias, sperm-whales
click dialects and Pacific grays drum
 poundings of chirp-like whistles.

At Navy's Submarine Surveillance,
the Navy increases sonar intensity until it ricochets
off the ocean floor.
One pod of whales, pups to elders cringe
close to shore, mill in circles in one direction
and then another,
become trapped in a cove.
All panic as they slap flukes against the water.

In every ocean an acoustic storm,
in every continent sonar-
depth charges on whales and dolphins leave
hundreds stranded en masse
in shallow waters, like castaways.

Hearing and navigation damaged,
unable to vocalize they can't locate mates.
A deaf whale is a dead whale!
Whale bellies lodge and twist in sand.
Devotees pour ocean water over them
and struggle to push them back. Sharks regroup.

Seasonal Changes

Fall
the world is rotating now
    I close the the windows and hearken
    to the chirps and rasps
    of grasshoppers, crickets and katydids
    and remember You.
 I sigh deeply,
     stargazers walk at midnight.
 I have heard
    serenading sounds of
    night come alive.
 I have felt
    your absence and your richness
    and have been blindfolded
    with losing you.
Clearing your created pool in the yard,
    I meditate on your precious breath.
My mind
    dreads the night chorus
    at full crescendo
    harbingers of winter and darkness.
And still
    a wild ringing
    and warblers getting a grip .
    The energy and joy of grandaughters and sons
    as hopeful as spring peepers.
    The waterfall in the back yard pond splashes.
I must bask
    with the sparrows that are left
    fill the feeders, pull the curtains open
    find my way of holding on.

Viewing "The Starry Night" by Vincent Van Gogh

Oh, hear the choirs of angels' melodies
playing in cosmic choreography,
tales they tell by starlight of ferris
wheels that spiral astray.
Aries vortex whirls in heaven's ballet.
There huddling below, San Remy town lies
guarded and mute, unaware of planet ties,
though linked to heaven by cypress trees
and the whirling planets cosmic rays.

See Mercury, the messenger make his way
to watch the great bear and little bear play.
See whirling dervishes of meteors commute
between strangers' stars and white dwarfs about.
See the dance of the planets, the crescent moon,
golden Venus, swirling bodies nascent.
There's Orion climbing that Robert Frost envisioned
and the wild, wild nights of Emily Dickinson.
Walk Van Gogh's tightrope strung out in light
As creation happens again with "The Starry Night."

After the Earthquake and Tsunami Roared Over Japan

How a pool filled with radioactive cesium
remains uncovered on a reactor building.
Space-suited workers click radiation detectors.
    How sparse the landscape as at Ground Zero
    with sarcophagi—as at Chernobyl.

How yellow vans turned over with bloated bodies inside,
        hundreds of cherry trees were uprooted
        fish and fowl fled belly up in ghost towns.

How tepees of twisted boards stand over graves
next to high-rise battered buildings.
    People were robbed of their sanity
    and others drenched in tears.

How a few Japanese workers returned to jobs a day after
found workplaces drowned in mud.
Mountains of debris stanched with dead sea things.
    There are towns no one can come back to.
    Street signs slashed in red on the ground.

How a solitary old couple walk down a sunken highway
Robots resemble human babies
and dolls mimic infant sounds for parents.
        Young adults retreat into an abyss of videos
        headed toward a void of homes and hearts
        shaded orange-red by the setting sun.

This Little Piggy

Dogs look up to you, cats look down on you. Give me a pig!
He looks you in the eye and treats you as an equal.

—Winston Churchill

I visit an industrial pig factory
where they are confined to gestation crates
with steel bars.
No trees,
no water or streams, no pastures,
no places to loll around.
Impregnated every month to give birth all their lives,
fed garbage and sewage.
Piglets, with tails cut off,
cry in pain for mothers.

Sows, boars and piglets
want to linger, grunt, snort, chomp, squeal,
clack their teeth and run around in open spaces.
Piglets wish to frolic, chase each other
find water to root in, and play with toys.

Yet, they see mates thrown
into dumpsters, killed,
hung up to bleed, confined, force fed,
and driven mad.

And we turn pigs into ham,
stuff and broil them, cook their ears,
deep fry them, make their heads into cheese
and pickle their feet.
Is not the flame of a new faith
rising from the sacrificial pigs?

Expedition to the Domain of Secrets in Papua, New Guinea

On the threshold of manhood, already
recognized as having been born with a canteen
of silver cutlery. He carried a continent in his soul.

And Lord, he took the long and crooked path
of a deep connection to the wind, water and land.
He knew and felt kinship with the natives

and frightening gods of natural elements.
He moved the country from its place and mapped
the course of outflowing rivers.

He trekked in knee deep mud and in the jungle learned
the magic of cassowaries, cuscus and wild pigs
and sang to red and green parrots, trying to find their nests.

Here natives, lost in time, wore human hair wigs
and pig tusks as jewelry. With yellow — painted faces
above grass skirts, they leaped, chanted, banged on drums

and carried human skulls of their fathers. Michael gave them
names he didn't reveal and announced
to the world their lives. At home his parents waited for news
that never came.

Into the brow of an age he enlightened us
about hunter gatherers' lives of warfare and head hunting.
Men shared wives, killed their neighbors, and ate their flesh.

He loved the land without any roads or cell towers,
crossed the mouth of the Betsj river where
his catamaran flipped over, he swam for shore and vanished.

Hammonasset Coast

Mid-morning fog lifts. My daughter and I
    bound together from different spheres,
        feel pull of moon on ocean's tide

on rocky outcrops heaving out of coast
    on cliffs where glaciers gouged retreat.
        We pause on pathway, sit on the bench

as my sister and I once did
    sharing Coleridge's,
        "The Rime of the Ancient Mariner."

Today dwellings slope to hidden beaches,
    and children explore tidal pools of slate-blue
        mussels and rosy crabs in flotillas

of seaweed. Wary of slick-covered
    downward slanting-boulders,
        a giant snail's trail, we view

the ocean's glow of cobalt blue
    writhing away to the horizon. My daughter's hair
        glistens with sunlight like my sister Beverly's

forty-five years ago. I breath the essence of wild roses
    and beach plums covering rocks.
        Crashing surf in high swells

sounds against domes of granite and schist.
    Hymns—emerge from shrubbery
        as swallow-tailed piping plovers wearing

black stripes on shoulders and brow
come soaring in on ocean tides
whistling their lonely notes.

Plovers flutter in circles and cuddle on rocky cliffs,
feathered wings clutching mates and chicks;
seeking green sea urchins that puff up spines

like porcupines. They anchor themselves to rocks
in ocean water, clear as a quartz crystal
flowing in tidal pools, most potent amber.

Wandering in Hammonasset Park

Above the shore, I watch the great white heron
with gigantic wing span envelop space,
ride the airwaves trailing its slender black legs.
In the moments between sunset and dusk
agile aviators, willets whistle over the sand hills.
A flock of piping plovers cut a dash,
defending their young on the upper shore
running back and forth pretending to be hurt,
trilling high notes.

Alone now, I remember the many times
we explored ocean bays and salt marshes:
collecting sculptures of sea shells,
surveying seals in the river
and once watched a Diamondback Terrapin cross our path.

At times, I close my eyes to hear the Fiddler Crabs' music.
Waves of silence between the requiem of the tide going out,
and the time before the last-light fading.

This is a world that dies, transforms and goes on
under a vast light-streaked sky.
The Hammonasset River twists and curves seeking
its ultimate outlet into the Sound
as air currents going out to sea pass over Rosa Rugosa.

Gathering American Chestnuts

By the stone wall, in its glory
a remaining American Chestnut thrives
in woodland soil spreading
and sheltering Indian paintbrushes, asters,
and forget-me-nots, going to seed underneath.

In November, we forayed into autumn woods
remembering long-gone summer's
pollen–bearing catkins and vanilla blossoms.

The grandest tree, tough, strong with brownish
bark offers a bounty of reddish-hued nuts.
We hurriedly collect them, tap, crack
and snack on some sweet interiors
equivalent to a confection,
of chocolate-covered cherries.

My other sister and I fill our baskets for cookies
and fudge. The maroon-colored chestnuts
are a blessing still remaining, the tree
not decimated when many have died.

Beyond the tree, a dim ghost, my sister across
the stone wall brings another basketful for us,
a part of our memories of Christmas treasures.

Now That She Is Gone

Out of the grave my younger sister
said, *my personal landscape has changed,*
forgive me for dying
so young and leaving you
to comfort and console
my three children and become their net
in anxiety's well.

I accepted my ex-husband's marriage to his student
and transcended it, though I couldn't
endure the cancer that abducted me.
I hope you see my life in that other universe
for the tangled orchard that it was
with the crab apples dropping and eaten
by the crows and starlings.

An Old Man's Reminiscences, 1845

Inspired by the landscape painting of Asher B. Durand,1796-1886

In August at the summit of my age, sitting
under the boughs of the oak tree one golden
afternoon, I watch small happenings hearing
    a melodic wood thrush.

Yet, still unfinished business, I'm like monarchs
and fritillaries taking three generations
to get to their butterfly homes. My body grips
    the sun-warmed earth.

I'm the man I didn't dream of becoming,
reminded of the kindness of family, lovers,
happy children playing in kaleidoscopes
    of trees and woods.

Nearby, the landscape, my trustful son brings
in a load of hay for Jerseys and Holsteins
as my farmland grows smaller. I see myself in him
and hear my father's and mother's voices
    deep within myself.

Still dragons ambush. I stumble forward holding
back a lot brushing aside complex feelings behind simple
questions that I don't know the answers to.

Why do they not listen to my stories?
I'm the mirror of the playing children. The river
of my desire goes on flowing and my veined hands
    are still capable.

Much pleasure comes from grandchildren
spreading their wings and the trees that harbor
newly hatched owls. I recall joys
        of youthful days.

Low autumn sun cuts through the trees, scintillating
on lovers, embodiments of sensual grace in stillness,
subtly erotic as I was in my troubadour years
        artful and uninhibited.

Letter to My Lover

How young you were at 25, just home from Korea
and I had never had a lover before.
You enticed me with charismatic ways.

Your cool shades, tailored suits and white shirts
with striped ties, until I bought you Jerry Garcia ones.
No one in the city dressed as you did.

Mister Right, Despite-Some-Quirks,
you didn't like Yankee food and made fun of it;
only your family's Italian cooking satisfied.

Still, grounded in genial and political humanity
you tossed off your grace notes holding me in thrall
with your kindnesses and friends.

So I would spend my paycheck on an Eiffel Tower tie
from Brook's Brothers and tailor a mint-green sport jacket for you
and we both preened for Saturday night soirees.

You rose fast in the hierarchy of New Haven, teaching,
giving out favors and jobs, becoming Commissioner,
setting off sparks like a modern Prometheus.

You gave a home to a snapping turtle and let out the raccoon
from a *Have A Heart* trap, planted for birds and created
a sanctuary like no other to dismiss the void of retirement.

Remember we curled together in one small bed
and I borrowed your fire and each day gained enlightenment
and every other year for six years birthed three babies.

Other layers: we travelled around the world
and floated the pontoon boat down the river in New Zealand.
At times we docked it and changed our directions.
All I want now is warmth for my bed
and to quiet the dread of your departure.

First Love

I follow too much the devices and desires of my own heart.

— Jane Kenyon

Over ammonium dichromate to make a chemical volcano
for 9th grade students, I met him.
Touchingly assertive, he gave me an illusion of relief
helping me to calm my students with his strength.
We were different, he Mediterranean, Italy,
I Atlantic Ocean, New England.
His deep azure eyes kindled sparks glowing
from within both of us. A glint of stars.
Then, he, the chemistry and physics
and alchemy of friendship and love.

After school, how fragrant and cool the cabernet
and chardonnay on the spring, expansive lawn.
In the evening, with naked feet digging in the grass,
we watched the mallards at Edgarton Park.
Heart in full bloom, my new closest friend,
in a single bed, Psyche and Eros.

The river flowed and meandered from my home.
The old trees in the park grew green and lush.
Bobolinks rose out of the hayfield spikes
and sang an evocative cacophony of melody.
Locked together, the ruling force
transformed our warm breath with sleep.

In the Evening

a balmy haze lies over West Cemetery
the newest in gravestones. A whispering
breeze shivers cinnamon ferns. For ten
months raw some memories have escaped
but today your beloved life demands attention.
Shapeless thoughts sink down in the soil.

The fragrance of silver-white bells permeates
the air, lilies-of-the valley, familiar
to me from childhood, dangle on delicate stems
in shade by your grave.

In this quiet field stretching onward,
stand decks of granite stones. I kneel
on newly shorn grass and read Frost's words:

I end not far from my going forth
By picking the faded blue
Of the last remaining aster flower
To carry again to you.

Interrupting my thoughts, a cemetery
dwelling creature sprints near me.
A warty toad, covered in dirt, puffs himself up
with unblinking eyes like the frogs you harbored
in our backyard pond.

Love Lies Bleeding

Blue-green algae
    in pond under running stream,
    nine green-spotted frogs meditate
    on lily pads. Rose-colored,
    scented crab apple blossoms
    umbrella overhead.

Land
    embroidered with yellow lilies
    hills and hollows
    broad rocks and boulders
    stranded head skeleton of dog or fox,
    pond-weedy, ground, sand, mulch.

I *pssh*, to flush birds from trees
    as a ruby-throated hummingbird, enticed
    from hydrangea beats its wings and hums
    in front of my lens.

Woodchuck announces his presence
    with a shrill alarm call;
    bull briar grasps my legs as I chase him.
A golden disk rules our loves
    but cinnamon fern glade loves shade.

Love Lies Bleeding, Lilies-of-the Valley,
    Showy Self-heal, Snow-on-the-Mountain
Dragon's Blood, Canterbury Bells,
    Forget-Me-Nots, Cathedral Windows,
    Love–in-the Mist and Bleeding Hearts.

He planted them all.

Forgetting How to Sing Without Him

There's a constant movement in my head,
like currents of the Bay of Fundy
off the North Atlantic Coast.
In the mists of ocean's spray, misty memories of him.
The Rose of Sharon reaches out curtsying
in skirts of lure.
I stand under the evening sky.
A wave of blues is on the loose.

I miss closing my eyes, touching,
knowing him there in bed beside me.
The walks along the boardwalk, Willard Island,
Meig's Point and Middle Beach before tropical storms,
the meteor showers and moon that shone
at Hammonasset under the evening sky. I profoundly
miss the memories he will never make, the remnants
of dreams unfulfilled, the call that won't come.
My hands touch the history books he read
and I can't take them off the shelves.

How determined he was to keep on mulching,
planting bulbs, building walls, and tending the gardens.
I miss his brusque voice rich with possibilities
but don't miss the in and out
of his hesitant breathing at night.
I wish he could have said good-bye with an embrace
but his heart gave up too soon.

How empty is the bedroom and back yard
where he labored a few months ago.
Pollen scatters into the air and the bull briars
are entangling and smothering the pine trees.
I trudge along revisiting the embroidered ground
slipping on moss-covered rocks, falling over myself
into the wild grape vines.

Sitting Outside Staring at Flowers

On an ancient wooden and metal bench
near jade bower overhung
with orange blossoms.
Hydrangeas in full rich velvet colors range

from pinkish-white to lavender, then deep-purple.
They throw out full crinolines of leaves and flowers.
Viburnams compete for showiness with spiky stalks
of burgundy blooms.

Peonies have dropped their exuberant petals,
now tinged with brown calligraphy.
Ruffs of deeply cut greenery of hosta,
and fox gloves' fairy, elfin thimbles
with dotted brown centers stand tall.

Walking sticks lure the scarce bumble bees.
Cinnamon ferns loving shade sway
with the Texas bluebells dancing in morning breeze.
Who planted and massaged these bountiful blooms?

 Bejeweled dragonflies skim over the pond.
All living metaphors proclaim the divine.
A splendid viewing place to await the next life.

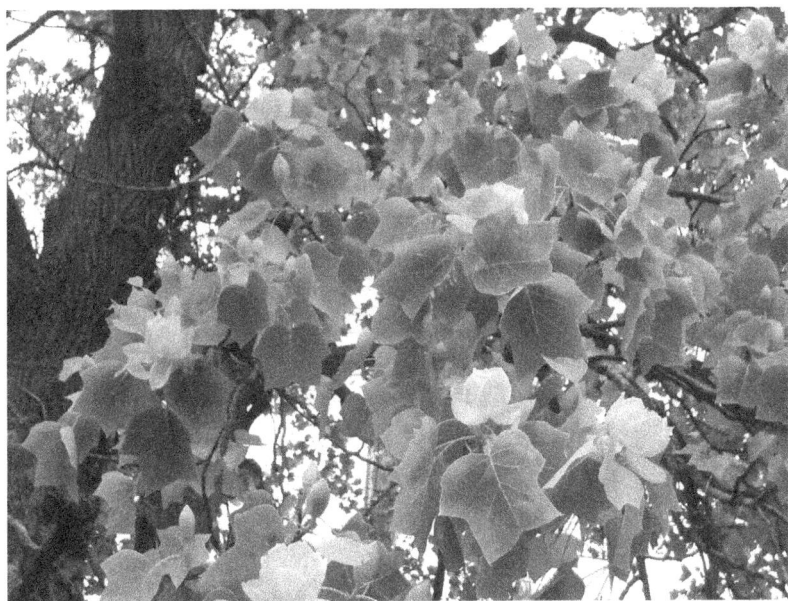

Fracking Despair

Drilling down into Marcellus layers of DNA around the clock,
a cloud of exhaust, like a windstorm in blood
invades once internal pasture land. Dust spreads
over the sun of his mind, acropolis of overturned earth,
crack open the shale. Layers of arms, legs
and bones bereave. A gargantuan machine
continues to dig a black hole deep into his earth
to shatter millions of cells, depopulating flesh,
desiccating lungs. Remaining energy releases
to trembling and shaking. Fear and anxiety leave him.
Strangled, the last breath quiets his chest.
Underground water strangles the last breath
quitting its chest.
Over his once strong shoulders, his pasture of wildflowers
scarred by blasting rock.

Dancing at Donahue's

The Flying Lotuses, Gregorian Chants and Wildcats
are gigging tonight and Mae Wok is the daredevil DJ.
The doorman greets and kisses the Mother Nature Witch
remarking, *you are becoming a regular here.*
Musicians trill electric guitars, harmonize the bass drum,
electrify the player piano and shimmer the sax,
incanting and riffing in a new world remix.
Get Rhythm, Johnny Cash's strain intensifies
the movement crashing together with Jerry Lee Lewis'
"Whole Lotta Shakin' Goin On."

Hip -hop dancers, set askew, tangle on the dance floor
like mantises evolving their gyrations in funk-jazz asides.
The band so percussive
with raw emotion and dance provocation intensifies.
Joining the flock, the wild woman dances shaking her hips
swinging her steps, intertwining her arms—carried away
with Rockabilly's thrill.
With the Fast Lane Band,
her hair escapes her butterfly clip
vines and tendrils dance around her neck .

The Nature Witch's body can rip it up,
gather vibes and rhythm into her soul.
She, pirouettes, wildly improvising,
pulsating upper body, moving to the beat.
Her footwork and legwork turn in and out,
staccato into legato.
It is the great night of the highwayman and the wanderer
of Ring of Fire when she thinks you will join her.

Kennewick Man Speaks Secrets after 9,000 Years

His skeleton found in the cold earth
in a bend of Columbia River. An archeologist
moved his bones, frail as Beleek china
and "spoke for him who could no longer speak."
Scientists cradled each bone piece and laid it out.

He led an eventful life. Ponder a list of possibilities.
The bones speak to me.
I imagine a husky man with a full beard,
a narrow skull and small face. Rugged and handsome
with weather-beaten long hair.
He was broad and strong, muscular
and tall, about 160 pounds.
One of his enemies left the spear point
embedded in his hip bone.

I think his closest relatives were the Moriori people
and the Japanese Ainu, hunter-gatherers
 of the North Pacific.
Anthropologists might have deduced that his mind,
heart and spirit widely roamed.
They learned that he lived on marine
animals and drank glacial water.

Observers noticed a skull fracture and broken
unhealed ribs. He used to throw spears
as a seal hunter.
He often pinched his fingers and thumb together
presumably chiseling spear points.
From dents in his cranium, anthropologists speculated
that he could have whirled a bola at birds.

Around forty years, death took him
from the people who esteemed the man
burying him with his head higher than his feet.

Learning to Dance with the Shakers

With a glimmer of salvation, the Sisters,
Prudence and Frances,
took me in to their community.
As I thought I was only going to spend a few days,
my suitcase was not very full.

I was ten years old when my mother died
from tuberculosis. That summer
my father couldn't take care of me.

Brother Arnold had just driven the sheep
into the barn, pitched hay to the cows
and horses and mucked out their stalls.
With his calloused brown hands,
he welcomed me and my father.
As days went by I began to think,
he was the Son of Heaven.

That first night I slept, not too deeply,
under a feathered quilt.
Sister Frances in bib-front dress woke me
at 5:30 am.

The Shaker lanterns gave a warm glow
as we sat silently at oblong tables for our
always-on- time meals.

Believing God, I lived this gospel
proclaiming it with dancing and writhing.

I slid into that embracing life
like diving into a clear trout stream,
a hummingbird sucking the nectar of flowers,
the mountain whippoorwills singing at night.

Last Year

Naturalist Journeys
took me to the miracle of the last true
wilderness of Alaska's Wildlife Preserve
where I hiked
on the coastal plains. I marveled at thousands
of porcupine caribou journeying 350 miles
from Yukon Territories
to the American Serengeti
migrating to spring calving on coastal plains
as the last herds of buffalo in the Midwest.

Here I met Gwich'in clans, *first on the land*
on snowshoes, sleds and birch bark canoes,
who told me their parables of the Boy in the Moon,
Wolf and the Wolverine and Caribou and the Fish.
Everything in their world possesses life force.
They believe that in the afterlife
flowers are thought to sing.

Inner Dresden

The mastered denial, the labored breathing,
a loan made for the cost
of a lung transplant.
The last ride home from Burlington,
giving clear directions on I 95. "Do not call
the ambulance! We need Michael,
not the paramedics." He wants his son.

The night he died, the Chevie truck's headlights
rose in the driveway. Then, he fell in the garage
on the cement floor.
His painted bunting colored eyes opened
questioningly.

Shrapnel cuts into my chest.
I give the kiss of breath
and feel the pale, cold skin.
I cannot shake the guilt
for his running out of oxygen.

I imagine that paramedics will revive
him. But I feel the heartburn
in my breast and fear that I will not see him
alive again.
The tailspin of grief pains like a phantom limb.

Later, I will give away the Henredon bed and bureau
and pack up all the bird sculptures and paintings.
Roll up the oriental rugs he loved.
The nature sanctuary sinks into an elegy of ghosts
and memories as the Dresden
of inwardness seizes me.

As I Ebb Toward...

I
On a painted bunting day
as the ferry pulls away from Nantucket,
I spy fish-wielding dolphins,
vaulting out of the sea.
Baby whales follow the songs
of their mothers
seeking milk from their breasts.
And a sperm whale floats in the waves.

II
Gray shingled houses look out
at waves rising and falling.
Around the bay, pink swamp mallows
frame the marsh, use underground
networks to share water
and call to their pollinators.
I stoop to touch mosaic of sea shells
on berm of sand

I'm swimming in the foam
as waves crest over my head and I float
on to the calmer seashore of Nantucket beach.
Flocks of storm petrels arc up and down and glide
like helicopters over waves.

III
My womb now empty once housed four lives.
Two survived into the baptism of life.
I have lost my place like stones on
the upper beach.

What do I have to latch onto
in the currents and the waves?
Isn't it enough to swim with spiraling surges?
The Great Point light anchors as holdfasts
of giant kelp suspend me.

Here's a Portrayal of a Woman I Know

She's sitting up in her bed reading,
All the Light We Cannot See.
In her night sky, gossamer rays unfold
in a shroud of mist as erratic as the wind.

She has survived losses too heavy to lift.

She is growing older, listening to spirits
and dreaming of the dead who send messages.
She hears her mother's voice saying
"It is forbidden!"
She'd rather listen to her father, a farmer
who planted trees and gardens.

Her husband had choreographed adventures
and coaxed her to play, extended
his Mediterranean light and a garden of flowers,
shared a kiss that has lasted this long.
Farewell my generous one, she often says.

She sees the sea as a Sacred Source
and the new moon move across the sky.

Retreat to the Cabin

I say let your affairs be as two or three, and not a hundred or a thousand;
instead of a million count half a dozen,
and keep your accounts on your thumb nail.

—Henry David Thoreau

I loosen my grip on the old homestead,
to move to a cabin without plants,
trees and flowers. Even the white spruce,
hawthorn and witch hazel I leave behind.

Unravel all I have built up
and collected for half a century,
shift amid myriad buttons of repair,
knobs, levers, and controls, as if playing an organ.

Dismantle the Japanese-Crown crane mural,
forget the bird bath buried by the frozen snow,
donate the family's antique clock to the church.
There is a phantasmal cloud moving, but still,

my new place a cavalcade of shooting stars.
At night, I see Orion's belt glimmer and point to Sirius.
I pull all the stops and hear the chorus of voices
play a Bach Trio Sonata.

Bald Cypress in Florida Park

On the Atlantic coastal plain for 3,500 years
echoing the voices of the aboriginals
before Disneyland rose out of the swampland.

Reddish-brown bark and tassel-like clusters
of flowers festooned with strands
of Spanish moss.
Out of the mud the cypress sent out
fluted-knee pinnacles.
Needles shimmered from green to gold
as it stood with sustaining breath
on the edge of the ridge

Resinous fragrance softening the air,
forged strength for butterflies
surviving migrations
and cast canopies for songbirds.
A passel of children holding hands
surrounded it.

Once struck by lightning it smoldered
slowly, then survived many logging assaults.
Not hurricanes, nor loggers could collapse it.

Until one morning, I came early
to its ancient altar
only to see its trunk split in half and chards
of wood thrown up around it burning
with pulsing fire.
Out of nowhere a broad-wing hawk circles
from the smoky clouds and inscribes
its loss.

Farmer Roscoe (The Philosopher) ca 1937
Painting by Ivan Olinsky
"Suggests man's attitude toward life and the soil."

When the sun crosses the vernal equinox
the fields bleached by snow
convert to islands
of brown green, cradled by the hills.

Every morning, I take out the heavy-boned horses
to pull the plow next to a little valley
and turn up the squirming earthworms.
I dig weeds and turn up rich-smelling
spadefuls of soil.
Then, I plant peas laying them out in rows
make grooves for cucumbers, squash,
carrots and lettuce.
Rabbits, woodchucks and raccoons steal
under the fences.

The sun warms deep into the earth
through branches of bare trees.
Sap begins to flow.

Birds migrate to breeding grounds:
meadows, woodlots, brooks and fields.
Warblers and hummers erupt from branches
and grace my farm with cascades
of twitters, trills and songs.
The winged gods of high places with eyes
like black pearls, glossy as midnight,
with fleeing silhouettes
scan for prey then vanish over the mountain.

Every night, after tilling, I tuck my work horses
in before I hand milk my cows
 feel my bones blaze and skin effervesce.
Yet, this farm is in my heart and issues into my mind
and my fanned hands over everything.
I do not learn to relinquish gracefully.

The Spirit Bear, Panda of Canada

In the Great Bear Rainforest, a crow sounds clarion
caws and alerts the animals to our arrival.
A glowing female bear, sacred to local tribes,
rare as the rarest Okapi shifts her weight of 300 pounds
and waddles out of the salmon river.

Numinous with full honey-hued hair,
she bats a pink salmon.
They are Kermodes belonging to the territory of the
        Kitasoo people.

Her first-year-of-life cub
sports a red fur collar and a white-brown coat.
There is no male to take it down so mother and cub slip

into the pool. The cub studies us curiously, sniffs us out
and devours the flesh of the batted salmon,
wrapped in sea weed. Mother eats the brains and eggs.

Silently snapping our cameras as for celebrities,
we wait frozen with rapture, flooded with reverence
for the legacy of mother and her cub.

Gingko, Oldest Surviving Plant

(Thousands of years-old lineage preserved
by Chinese monks in ancient groves of monasteries.)

Nestled among oak and beech
with its canopy of elegant fan-shaped leaves,
the male grand sage towers over stream side.
This ultimate survivor tree shimmers

with green and apricot-gold leaves
below silver halos. When the leaves
drop, darkness lengthens and the sun sinks
toward the horizon.

I wish to delve down into its labyrinth of roots
and find its generative force
that has survived volcanic eruptions, asteroid
collisions and Hiroshima's catastrophe.

Like a character from *Hitchhiker's Guide to the Galaxy*
I imagine secrets unraveling in treetops and roots.

Finding the Gingko Tree

Because it holds the generative core of life, we can
    learn from it. Nourished by spring rains and sunbaths
        it radiates
          a redolence of rays.
      Male sperm cells wiggle and swim from catkins,
        make their way to the female tree
    and join ovaries   .

  Saved by Buddhist monks o the island of Deshima
        Green-gray lichen and reindeer moss home in
  on the bark.

Silver-apricot colors the lobed fan-shaped leaves.

  Some lived on after the atomic blast of Hiroshima
    near the epicenter of the explosion
    "No More Hiroshimas" carved on one's temple.

Golden leaves nourish the inner tree, keep it alive through stormy
    seasons
and hide the tiny nest of a ruby-throated hummingbird
    interwoven
        with thistledown, its life-saving defense.
Maidenhair glows in the dark when the sun is gone.

The Lost Girls, Men and Babies

Based on painting Jaipur by Noemia Barroqueiro

I'm robbed of child, Laila, baby Abu and husband Omar.
This hijab covers my scabs, wounds and bony
shoulder blades.
When my babies were born the whole town joined
in celebration, rippled with gratitude and laughter.
Now my heart is ravaged. Savages sliced off
my husband's head. My babe killed in my arms.
We are the sisterhood and brotherhood
of chaos, loss and brutal violence.
Even hyenas writhe in agony.

After kidnapped, I slept outdoors
fighting snakes and scorpions, starved
and had to forage for plants to eat.
The guerrillas of Islamic State,
marched me to a hideout cave
in the ancient volcanic mountains
with hundreds of other women
and children to become
suicide bombers.

I can't imagine what kind of god
would want this killing.
I can't believe what kind of god would want you in heaven.
after all your killing and sins against humanity.

Land shifts and seasons change and
a cascade of asteroids blasts the earth.
The moon spins and the sun sets still.
A black night is all encompassing.

Oh Taliban, ISIS and Boko Haram what have we done
that makes us slaves of grief and violence?
I scream for the tsunami to come and drown you.
Lost love makes a monsoon in the soul.

His Story at Eighteen

Late at night, my stepmother and father
watched as a burly Jamaican and a tattooed
man lured me to the back seat of an SUV
and tied me down.
I did not know where I was going.

Did they wave as I was driven away, nine hours
to Ogdensburg, crying?

At the Academy, I was the youngest boy
at fourteen--sometimes force fed, pinned
 on the ground, locked alone in a room.
At night I could not have my shoes.
I couldn't go to sleep, buried my head
in the pillow trying to smother.

One night, when the big guys rioted, set fires,
broke up and threw furniture out the windows
of the classrooms.
The principal called us
"combustible characters,"
to the state police
and United States Border Patrol
who put down the uprising, spraying us
with tear gas and putting shackles
on the rioters.

Five years later in nightmares,
I wake up from being tied down,
hiding from hovering bullies, hear alarms,
and smell sulphur of tear gas....

Remaining Destination

In memory of Alicia and Frank

As we assemble around the Bermuda Cruise table:
a convergence of parents, children and grandparents,
two empty places. One son missing stretching
toward success working the land
with shovel, plow and spade
and our grandson.

Jake's mother, the wellspring of joy for all of us —
who left us last year.
Her sweet breath mingles with the wild flowers
of lady slippers, trilliums and New England asters.
The earth rejoices.

Grandfather breathes a serene expression
of *universal grief* and sincere gratitude
for the remaining family.
We remember his antipasto and seafood linguine
that he used to prepare
for the Feast of the Seven Fishes.

I lean against Frank's arm and prayerful
folded hands. We coalesce around him
lost in the chaotic abyss of missing
an only beloved daughter.

An echo of meadowlarks singing music
as the moon peeks into the dark interior.
Here is the small banquet
we are blessed to accept.

Acknowledgements:

Grateful acknowledgement is made to the editors of the following journals in which poems have appeared, some in slightly rewritten versions:

Whisper in the Woods: Michigan's Nature Journal, Winter 2004, Anthology of New England Writers, 1998, Connecticut Journal, 1995, Connecticut River Review, 1995, Connecticut Review, 1998, Eclectic Rainbows, Family Earth, Southern Connecticut Folio, Monadnock, Moose Bound Press, Massachusetts Journal of Graduate Liberal Studies, Oregon Poetry Journal, Poetry Forum, The Connecticut Writer, The Lowell Pearl, Tributaries, Verse Weavers, Oregon State Poetry Anthology of Prize Winning Poems, A Journal of Nature Writing, Caduceus, 2004, 2005, Poetics, 2004, 2008, Writers Unlimited , Golden Words, 2005-2006, California Poetry Journal, 2005, 2008, 2009, Long River Run II, 2006, Connecticut River Review, 2008, Connecticut Poetry Society Review, 2008, 2009, "Connecticut Senior Poets Laureate Honor Scroll Award," Angels Without Wings ,2009, 2010, 2014, CT Review 2013, 2014.

Poetry Awards

Recipient of Robby Garbo Award, Southern Connecticut State
        University, 1991

Graduate Poet of the Year, SCSU, 1991

First Prize, Kentucky State Poetry Society, "In Beijing, There Are
        No Dawn Redwoods,"1991

First Prize, Kentucky State Poetry Society, "Climbing," 1991

First Prize, Blowing Leaf Poetry Contest, "The Loons Call," 1995

First Prize, Poet's Roundtable of Arkansas, "Lake District's Dry
        Stone Walls," 1994

Second Prize, Kentucky State Poetry Society, "The Loons Call";
        "Wilderness Champion," 1995

Second Prize, Indiana State Federation of Poetry Clubs, "Gondola
        Lifted Us" 1995

First Prize, California Poetry Society, "In Beijing…" 1996

First Honorable Mention, *Explanations* for "Elegy for Rachel
        Carson" and On the Lawn at Crest Haven," 1996

First Honorable Mention, Indiana State Federation of Poetry
        Clubs, "You Can Hear the Jaguars Cry at Night," 1996

First Honorable Mention, *Writer's Unlimited*, "Luck" 1997

First Prize *Nature's Tributaries*, "The Commander and the Spotted
        Owls,"1998

First Honorable Mention, Women in the Arts Spring Contest,
        "Chimps in Gombe Park" and "Hiking England's Lake
        District," 1998

Second Prize, California State Poetry Society, "Bienvenido Perez
        Turbi," 1998

Silver Laureate Award of Senior *Poets Poetry Competition*,
        2005-2006

First Prize, California State Poetry Society Contest, "Riding the
        Chariot to the Divine," 2006

First Prize, Al Savard Memorial Poetry Contest for Connecticut
        Poets, "Libretto for Spirit Bear of British Columbia," 2006

Poetry Awards

First Prize, *Northern Lights*, "Caring for the Land," 2007

First Honorable. Mention, Morgantown Poetry Society, "Backyard Tulip Tree, 2007

First Prize, Pennsylvania Yearly Poetry Contest, "Lake District's Dry Stone Walls," 2008

Third Prize, Pennsylvania Poetry Society, "Metamorphosis," 2008

Third Prize, Connecticut Poetry Society, "Orca's Opera," 2008

Senor Poet Laureate Award, 16th Annual National Senior Poets Laureate Poetry Competition for American Poets for Best Poem, "Tonight," 2008

High Prairie Poets, Third Place, "Whales," 2008

Second Prize, California State Poetry Contest, "Twenty-Seven Degrees Warmer," September, 2008

Third Prize, California State Poetry Contest, '"The Landscape of Loss," October, 2008

Third Prize, Connecticut State Poetry Society Contest, "Libretto for Spirit Bear Wilderness," June, 2008

Second Place, "The Day After the Six Year War," January 20, 2009.

Second Place, CT Poetry Society, "Shackleton's Voyage", April, 2009

Life Press National Poetry Awards: Second Place, "God's Country" 2009

Connecticut Senior Poets Laureate Honor Scroll Award, "Alicia, to My Daughter" 2009

Grandmother Earth National Award; "The Loons Call"

Second Place, California State Poetry Society, "Fairy Penguins at Phillip's Island, Australia," August 2009

First Prize, Oregon State Poetry Society, 2010 for "Landscape of Loss"

2005-2006, Silver Laureate Award: "Angels Without Wings"

2008, Senior Poet Laureate

Poetry Awards

2009, Senior Poet Laureate--Honor Scroll Award
2012, Senior Poet Laureate--Honor Scroll Award
2012, California State Poetry Society--Honorable Mention for
      "Great- Horned Owl Family"
2014, Connecticut Poetry Award, Second Place for Farm Poem
2014, Second Prize, Old Saybrook Poetry Contest for "Love Lies
      Bleeding"

Carol was awarded the degree of advanced Study at Wesleyan University, after receiving a Master's Degree in English and American literature and Sixth Year Degree in Educational Leadership at Southern Connecticut State University. While there, she received "Graduate Poet of the Year."

As recipient of an English Speakers Union's Scholarship, Carol has studied English literature and culture at the University of London for two summers and participated in Yale/New Haven Teachers Institute for six years.

A member of the Guilford Poets Guild, she is now a retired English and science teacher. She has published five previous books of poetry: *In Beijing; There Are No Dawn Redwoods, Isinglass River, The Jade Bower, Still Brooding on a Strong Branch* and *Chronicles of Humans with Nature. Parables of Passages* is the sixth one.

Aside from spending time working for protecting natural resources of Hammonasset State Park and Biological Reserve, participating in Shoreline Institute of Lifelong Learning, she writes memoirs and takes classes in poetry workshops with Guilford Poetry Guild. In addition, she enjoys her grandchildren, hiking, birding, traveling, and reading: natural history, novels, traditional and contemporary poetry, and creative non-fiction. Also, she is interested in photography to illustrate her nature and human poems. She recently won a State of Connecticut Green Circle Award for environmental activism.